THE TRAGEDY OF
KING
CHRISTOPHE

THE TRAGEDY OF
KING
CHRISTOPHE

a play by

Aimé Césaire

*translated
from the French
by Ralph Manheim*

GROVE PRESS, INC.
NEW YORK

THE TRAGEDY OF
KING
CHRISTOPHE

CHARACTERS

HENRI CHRISTOPHE   former slave, former cook, former general, King of Haiti

MADAME CHRISTOPHE   former servant, the Queen

VASTEY   Baron, secretary to Christophe

CORNEILLE BRELLE   Duke of the Cove, first archbishop of the Cape

MAGNY   Duke of Pleasance, general

PÉTION   President of the Republic

GUERRIER   General, duke

MARTIAL BESSE   French engineer

HUGONIN   a combination of parasite, buffoon, and political agent

RICHARD   Count of the Northern Marches

STEWARD   Christophe's Scottish physician

METELLUS   a conspirator

JUAN DE DIOS   Archbishop of the Cape after the death of Corneille Brelle

Citizens, courtiers, deputies, peasants, soldiers, workers, ladies

Scene: Haiti, 1806–1820

The Tragedy of King Christophe was first performed by the Europa Studio at the Salzburg Festival, Salzburg, Austria, August, 1964, directed by Jean-Marie Serreau.

Prologue

THE COCK FIGHT

~~~~~~

Six to eight PEASANTS, *standing around the arena, leaning forward. When they speak, they look up at the audience. The cocks are represented by feathers moving to and fro.*

CRIES: Here dey come!

CROWD: Sharpen yuh knuckles, fellas. De better cock mus' tell today.

THE REFEREE: Cocks mus' fight till death. No doping allowed. The battle! Pétion versus Christophe!

A VOICE: Silence!

CRIES: Go fuh yuh man, Christophe.

A VOICE: Take 'im early, Christophe.

A VOICE: Make 'im chase you, Pétion. Hit, run, and weave.

A VOICE: Dis looks to be a stalemate. Seems like dey been rubbed with snake oil.

VOICE: Lick him, Christophe, kill 'im.

VOICE: Use the ground, Pétion . . . more . . . more.

VOICE: He's sprawled over, he's licked.

VOICE: Ref! Make Pétion fight. He's faking. Stand 'im up.

VOICE: Faking, eh!! Down is not out, far more dead.

VOICE: Wash 'is ass with nettle.

VOICE: Inject 'im. Dat will take de scare out o' 'im.

VOICE: Fake! Farce! Thief! Thieving! Pétion's an ole hen.

VOICE: Get away! He's an A-1 fighter! Rub 'im wid
    ginger.
CROWD: Bring 'im to 'is senses.
VOICE: Time to fight back, Pétion ... Fight ...
CROWD: Wash 'im, Christophe.
VOICE: Boy oh boy.
VOICE: Mother, what a poke in the eye!
CROWD: Hurrah! Hurra-a-a-h!

THE COMMENTATOR *enters and goes front stage. He
is dressed like a European gentleman of the period.
The* PEASANTS *remain on the stage, but the light
shifts to* THE COMMENTATOR:

THE COMMENTATOR: Fighting cocks used to have names
like Drum Major or Peck-'is-Eye-Out; today they are
named after political figures: in this corner Christophe, over there Pétion. It didn't appeal to me at
first, but come to think of it, it's no more unrea-
sonable than most fashions. A King and a President
of the Republic are bound to tear each other's eyes
out. And if they tear each other's eyes out, why not
name fighting cocks after them? ... But, you may
argue, it's all very simple with fighting cocks, rela-
tions between men are more complicated. Not nec-
essarily. The main thing is to understand the situation and to know the men the cocks were named
after. Who is Christophe? Who is Pétion? That's
what I'm here to tell you.
    On the island of Haiti, formerly a French colony
called Saint-Domingue, there lived, early in the nine-
teenth century, a black general. His name was Christophe, Henri Christophe, Henri with an *i.*
    No, he hadn't started out as a general. He'd been
a slave, to be exact, a cook (what was known in
Saint-Domingue as a "skilled black.") Well, then,

this Christophe was the chef at the Sign of the Crown. (Remember that name, it was coined by fate.) The Sign of the Crown was an inn in the city of Cap Haitien, then called French Cape.

Christophe fought the French, playing an eminent part in the struggle for the liberation of his country, under the leadership of Toussaint Louverture. Once independence had been gained and Haiti was born from the smoldering ashes of Saint-Domingue, once a black republic had been established on the ruins of the fairest of white colonies, it was only natural that Christophe should become one of the dignitaries of the new state. He became, in all his glory, General Christophe, the much feared and highly respected commander of the Northern Province. Consequently, at the death of Dessalines, of Dessalines the founder, the first Haitian chief of state, all eyes turned to Christophe. He was appointed President of the Republic. But as I have said, he was a cook, in other words, a shrewd politician, and as a cook, he felt that the dish they were offering him was short on seasoning, that this presidency was rather a hollow honor. Abandoning the city of Port-au-Prince to the mulattoes and to Pétion, their leader, he set himself up in the Northern Province. From then on, to make a long story short, two states coexisted in Haiti, and none too peacefully: in the South a republic, with Pétion as president, in the North a kingdom.

There's the situation: Christophe and Pétion, two great fighting cocks, two calojies, as they say in the islands.

Yes, Christophe was King.

King like Louis XIII, Louis XIV, Louis XVI and a few others. And like every king, every true king,

every white king I mean, he created a court and sur·
rounded himself with a nobility.

But now I've said enough.

I give you Christophe, I give you Pétion.

Act 1

SCENE ONE

~~~~~~

When the curtain rises, PÉTION *is alone on the stage, pacing back and forth. He is holding a scroll.* CHRISTOPHE *enters. They greet one another with great ceremony.*

PÉTION: Upon you as Toussaint Louverture's old companion in arms, as the highest ranking general of the Army, the Senate unanimously confers the office of President of the Republic. (*He hands* CHRISTOPHE *the scroll, which* CHRISTOPHE *sniffs at from time to time but does not unroll.*)

CHRISTOPHE: The law is explicit, I am indeed entitled to the office. But what the constitution of the Republic gives me, an amendment voted under conditions of doubtful legality takes away. The Senate appoints me President of the Republic because it might be dangerous to rub me the wrong way. But it drains the presidency of all substance and my authority of all vigor. Yes, gentlemen, I know your Constitution. Christophe would be nothing but a big harmless jack-of-the-clock, with a toy sword, entertaining the populace by striking the hours of your law on the clock of his own helplessness.

PÉTION: You are unjust to the Senate. You'll always find flies in the ointment if you look too closely. The office we are offering you still has luster and importance. It is the highest in the Republic. As to the changes the Senate has seen fit to make in the

Constitution, I won't deny that they curtail the President's powers, but you can hardly be unaware that there is one danger which a people that has had to live under Dessalines fears more than any other. Its name is tyranny. The threat of it is still hanging over our heads. In my opinion it would have been unforgivable in the Senate not to take due precautions against that danger.

CHRISTOPHE: I'm not a mulatto, I don't sift my words. I'm a soldier, an old master-at-arms, and I'll speak plainly: the Senate's amendment to the Constitution is an expression of distrust in me, in my person. My dignity will not let me accept it.

Damn it, Pétion, what you're offering me in the name of the Republic is a position without flesh or bones, the scraps and leftovers of power. (*He drops the scroll and kicks it in walking.*)

PÉTION: I am sorry if I have failed to make myself clear. I've been speaking of principles, and you persist in talking about your own person. But we can't argue forever. Is this the answer you wish me to carry back to the Senate?

CHRISTOPHE: Wouldn't Pétion be glad to take me at my word?

PÉTION: What do you mean by that?

CHRISTOPHE: Pétion is intelligent, very intelligent. He can't help thinking that if Christophe declines the presidency it will be offered to Pétion.

PÉTION: Damnation, why would I accept what you disdain? If it's a bitter crab-apple to you, why would it be a juicy pear to me?

CHRISTOPHE: Because Pétion is intelligent. Very intelligent. The instant the mulatto Pétion accepts the empty power you have been offering me, a miracle will come to pass. Our friends of the Senate, the mulattoes of Port-au-Prince, will play the good fairies and presto chango, they'll fill his bowl to the brim. Take it, Pétion, take it, you'll see, it will be a horn of plenty.

PÉTION: Then you think . . . ?

CHRISTOPHE: I think the amendment to the Constitution is nothing but a crude trick to keep me out of power while pretending to make me chief of state.

PÉTION: And you mean to stand aside?

CHRISTOPHE: Hell and damnation! Stand aside! (*Laughs.*) Oh no, Pétion. When you teach a monkey to throw stones, there's a good chance he'll pick one up and bash your head in. Hm. Not bad. That's my message to the Senate. They'll know what I mean.

PÉTION: The Senate will know that the sender of such a message has ceased to be anything more than a rebellious general.

CHRISTOPHE: That's neither here nor there. If you want an official answer, a noble answer, the kind that will appeal to our Solons and Lycurguses of Port-au-Prince, tell them I regret that at a time like this their spirit of animosity toward my person should blind them to the greatest need of this country, of this people which must be protected, which must be disciplined, which must be educated. And that need is . . .

PÉTION: Freedom.

CHRISTOPHE: Freedom yes, but not an easy freedom. Which means that they need a State. Yes, my philosopher friend, something that will enable this transplanted people to strike roots, to burgeon and flower, to fling the fruits and perfumes of its flowering into the face of the world, something which, to speak plainly, will oblige our people, by force if need be, to be born to itself, to surpass itself. There is the message, rather too long no doubt, which I charge my obliging friend to convey to our noble friends in Port-au-Prince. (*Drawing his sword and advancing front stage, in a violent tone contrasting with his preceding calm.*)

And now: my sword and my right!

PÉTION *picks up the scroll and exits. Darkness.*

SCENE TWO

A public square in Cap Haïtien. View of the bay. Ships
on the horizon. Market women. Groups of citizens, with
whom mingle agents of CHRISTOPHE, among them HU-
GONIN. As the curtain rises, a woman steps forward and
sings in languid West Indian style:

> In the sea
> It wasn't me
> Who sank the skiff
> With the police
>
> In the sea
> It wasn't you
> Who sank the skiff
> With the police
>
> In the sea
> The Devil did that
> For you and me.
>
> Yes, Satan
> Sank the skiff
> Police and all.

MARKET WOMAN: Rapadou! Sugar lumps. This way for
everything your heart desires. Tafia. Rum. Tobacco
twists. Tobacco braids. Tassó! Tassó! Strips of beef.
(Addressing HUGONIN.) Have some sugar candy,
daddy?

HUGONIN: Hiya, honey. I'm not looking for candy,

you're the sugar for me. No strips of beef. How
about stripping you?

MARKET WOMAN: Bad boy! You mind your manners.
Flying fish! Kuku! Kuku! This way, gentlemen, get
your corn meal mush. Corn meal mush!

HUGONIN: My trouble is I only want to mush with you.

MARKET WOMAN: You no-good scamp! Help, police!

FIRST CITIZEN (*sitting on a crate off to one side. Speaks
to everyone and no one*):   You'll have to admit it's
curious. That ship that keeps turning up at the har-
bor mouth, and every time they send her back.

HUGONIN (*comes over to him and jostles him a little*):
You playing dumb? You don't know what that ship
is? (*Singing*):

That's old Mister Whale
Under that white sail
Watch out, watch out for Mister Whale
He'll bite your head off without fail.

Free translation: That ship belongs to the King of
France. And I'll tell you something else: if you need
whips for your lumbago, they've got plenty in the
hold.

FIRST CITIZEN: Sir!

HUGONIN: And if your backside wants to be cut up into
stewmeat, likewise. In that ship's hold they've got
just what your backside is asking for.

FIRST CITIZEN: Let's not exaggerate, sir. Perhaps they've
come to suggest an understanding. After all, why
not, if it can save the country from further commotion.

HUGONIN: Isn't that lovely! Your worship has a weak
heart. Your worship dislikes commotion. My poor
friend, understandings won't help. And neither will
your caution or cowardice. Just as some women are
given to falling sickness, and it comes over them at

any place or time, there are countries given to commotion, to convulsions, and ours is one of them.
That's its nature. Do you understand? No, you don't
understand. Never mind.

Four or five COURTIERS *enter, among them* VASTEY.

VASTEY: Get along, citizens. Go home. That ship is
none of our business. It's Christophe's business.
Each man to his trade. Yours is work, free work, for
you are free men, free to work for your country that
is in danger. Christophe's is to protect us, our persons, our property, our freedom.

SECOND CITIZEN: Well spoken! Christophe, yes. That's
a man, he's got what it takes. He's not a drag-ass
like Pétion. I hear that Pétion's offered to pay the
former colonials an indemnity in return for recogni-
tion by the King of France. Think of that! A Negro
offering to indemnify the people whom Negroes
have imprudently deprived of the privilege of own-
ing Negroes. (*He laughs bitterly.*)

HUGONIN: What are you complaining about? You know
the song:

> I'll sell you my cow
> Good butter, good milk
> And she'll calve in the spring
> For a dish of cod.
> I need a meal
> I need it now
> Then it's a deal
> You've bought my cow.

VASTEY (*casually*):   Christophe is a man, yes. All the
same, he's partly to blame for the situation, though
obviously not as much as Pétion.

SECOND CITIZEN: Watch your step, sir. Some compari-
sons are offensive . . . Offensive and dangerous.

VASTEY (*patiently*):   It's you, citizen, who had better watch your step. You will agree that the French—and it makes for a dangerous situation—hold us in low esteem.

FIRST CITIZEN: Naturally, because we're black.

VASTEY: Yes and no. Listen carefully. What are the white people in France saying? That Pétion and Christophe are both weaklings. The French, you see, have no respect for republics. Napoleon proved that. And what's Haiti? It's not even one republic, but two. Two republics, sir.

FIRST CITIZEN: That's a fact . . . But what can we do? Heavens alive, what can we do?

VASTEY (*raising his voice as though haranguing the crowd, which gathers around him*):   The whole world is watching us, citizens, and the nations think that black men have no dignity. A king, a court, a kingdom, that's what we've got to show them if we want to be respected. A leader at the head of our nation. A crown on the head of our leader. Believe me, that will quiet the military philanthropists who think we need their kind of order.

At this moment CHRISTOPHE *appears, preceded by a drummer and accompanied by four or five more* COURTIERS. SOLDIERS *march in, followed by a crowd.*

THE CROWD: Long live Christophe!

HUGONIN: Long live the man Christophe!

THE CROWD: Long live King Christophe!

CHRISTOPHE: That'll do! What kind of a nation is this whose only national occupation is gossiping! Haitian people! Haiti has less to fear from the French than from itself. This people's enemy is its indolence, its effrontery, its hatred of discipline, its self-indulgence, it's lethargy. Gentlemen, for the honor and survival of this nation, I don't want it ever to be said, I won't have the world so much as suspect, that ten years of black freedom, ten years of black slovenliness and indifference, have sufficed to squander the patrimony that our martyred people has amassed in a hundred years of labor under the whip. You may as well get it through your heads this minute that with me you won't have the right to be tired. Very well, gentlemen. Disperse.

THE CROWD: Long live Christophe!

HUGONIN: Long live the man Christophe!

THE CROWD: Long live King Christophe!

All exit. Darkness.

SCENE THREE

At the palace. THE MASTER OF CEREMONIES and three COURTIERS are wearing court trousers but are otherwise in a state of undress.

THE MASTER OF CEREMONIES: Come, come, gentlemen. Forgive me for rushing you, but the King will be here any minute. We really have to begin our rehearsal. I shall call the roll and review the general principles of the ceremony. It is a ceremony of the utmost importance, gentlemen. The whole world has its eyes on us.

The three COURTIERS *step forward and bow to each other in a little ballet of greeting. Meanwhile* VASTEY *enters, followed by* MAGNY.

FIRST COURTIER: Your Grace!

SECOND COURTIER: Your Lordship!

THIRD COURTIER (*tittering*): Oh, Your Excellency!

General laughter.

Two lackeys bring in a trunk and set it down rear. During the following, until THE MASTER OF CEREMONIES *calls the roll, some twelve* COURTIERS *enter by twos and threes, rummage in the trunk, take out festive garments, try them on and exchange them.* THE MASTER OF CEREMONIES *supervises their dressing.*

FIRST COURTIER: My goodness! This king, this kingdom, this coronation, I can't believe it.

SECOND COURTIER: You can't believe it, but you can feel it in your bones. It's backbreaking.

VASTEY: A black king! It's like a fairy tale, isn't it? This black kingdom, this court, a perfect replica in black of the finest courts the Old World has to offer.

MAGNY (*Duke of Pleasance*): My dear Vastey, I'm an old soldier. I fought under Toussaint and Dessalines, and frankly, I can't get used to these courtly ways that you seem to find so delightful.

VASTEY (*with great dignity*): My dear colleague! Magny! I never expected to hear such words from you, the Duke of Pleasance.

SECOND COURTIER: What do we look like with these high-sounding titles of ours, Duke of Lemonade, Duke of Marmalade, Duke of Candytown? My goodness, the French must be in stitches.

VASTEY (*ironic*): O man of little faith! (THE MASTER OF CEREMONIES *looks at* VASTEY *with approval during this speech.*) Come, come. Let the French laugh. Marmalade, why not? What's wrong with Lemonade? Those are names that tickle the palate! Gastronomic names! After all, the French have their Duke of Bouillon, the English have their Duke of Yorkshire Pudding! Are they any more appetizing? So you see, there are precedents. But seriously, Magny. Whom did Europe send us when we applied to the International Technical Aid Organization for assistance? Not an engineer. Not a soldier. Not a professor. A master of ceremonies. Form is what counts, my friend. That's what civilization is . . . the forming of man. Think it over. Form is the matrix of being, of substance, in short, of man himself. Of everything. It's empty, yes, but what a stupendous, generative, life-giving emptiness!

MAGNY: Sounds like pretentious rubbish to me.

HUGONIN *enters carrying a swagger stick and goes from one to the other, listening.*

VASTEY: There's one man who understands it instinctively. That's Christophe. With his great potter's hands, kneading the Haitian clay—he may not know, but what's more important, he feels, he smells the sinuous line of the future, in a word, the form. Believe me, that's something in a country like ours.

MAGNY: Damn your esthetic foolishness! If he'd taken my advice, instead of having himself anointed with cocoa oil, instead of having a crown put on his head, he'd have buckled on his sword and led us to Port-au-Prince, where there's so much fine land to take and so many scoundrels to shorten by a head.

HUGONIN (*pokes his swagger stick in Magny's chest*): I'm not a saber rattler. . . . Far from it. Or a beribboned minister of state. . . . But all the same, I've got my ideas on the subject. . . . It was brilliant . . . brilliant, do you hear . . . inventing a nobility. Now the King can baptize anybody he likes, he can be everybody's godfather. I'll admit that if the husbands let him, he wouldn't be every Haitian's godfather, he'd be their father. If I were a minister, I'd have a little suggestion for the King.

MAGNY: That's what we've come to, Vastey. A court, a nobility . . . and now the king's jester.

HUGONIN: Ho ho, it's raining titles. Upon my soul, that one's as good as another. I accept it, I welcome it. Well, here's my first try. You've heard about the baby boy that a certain portly lady has had by the King. Why not baptize him the Duke of Variety?

The COURTIERS *laugh violently, some rolling on the ground. Then they pick themselves up shamefacedly and straighten their clothes.*

VASTEY: Riddles may be our national sport, but that one surpasses my understanding.

HUGONIN: You see, you don't know everything. But take care! Here he is . . . Hell! I've got an itch in the small of my back.

The COURTIERS *improve their posture.*

THE MASTER OF CEREMONIES (*catching sight of* CHRISTOPHE):   Gentlemen, I beg of you, gentlemen, be silent. I shall proceed to call the roll. (HUGONIN *stands by the trunk and hands each one a hat corresponding to his rank*):

His Grace the Duke of Lemonade
His Grace the Duke of Pleasance
His Lordship the Marquis of Downwind
His Grace the Duke of Fatso
His Grace the Duke of Marmalade
His Grace the Duke of Candytown
His Lordship the Count of Stinkhole.

Equerries:
Jean-Louis Lamour
Bobo Cemetery
Jean-Jacques Severe
Etienne Register
Hercules Cupid
Joseph Almanzor

Officers of the Royal Dahomey:
Sir Jupiter
Sir Pierre Pompey
Sir Lolo Prettyboy

The two LACKEYS *remove the trunk and bring in an enormous chair, the back emblazoned with a sun, for* CHRISTOPHE.

Good, we are all present. Sir Leeward, master of the storeroom, will you kindly prepare the royal ornaments . . . Permit me to remind you that the order of presentation is as follows: the ring, the sword, the mantle, the hand of justice, the scepter.

Proceed, gentlemen.

CHRISTOPHE (*enters in brilliant uniform. Looks around*): Good, good. Splendid. But what a depressing shortage of women. Bring in the ladies, assign them their places in the ceremony. (*The* LADIES *enter: fullbodied black women, dressed fit to kill. They curtsey to* CHRISTOPHE, *who taps some of them on their rear ends as they pass.*) Come along, ladies, come along, my dear duchesses and countesses. (*The* LADIES *take their places.*) Lady Syringe . . . Lady Tidbit . . . Lady Easter Parade . . . my dear old friend!

After Christophe's greeting each one goes rear and returns with a CAVALIER. *The couples form a procession.*

MASTER OF CEREMONIES: Your carriage, ladies and gentlemen. Watch your carriage. Let's not have angular, spasmodic movements . . . Well-rounded gestures, that's what we need. Neither the stiffness of a soldier on the drillground nor the slovenly abandon of African feet and Creole arms. Let your manner be both dignified and natural . . . natural and solemn . . .

CHRISTOPHE (*exploding*): Damnation! Who cursed me with such a lot of slobs . . . Good Lord, Stinkhole. Stop shuffling! It's as if you were to address me disrespectfully. (*Taking* CANDYTOWN *by the collar*) . . . Is that a way to hand me the scepter? I'm not going to eat you. (*Turning to* VASTEY.) He looks as if he were giving an elephant a banana. (*General laughter.*)

MASTER OF CEREMONIES: Gentlemen, let's make a fresh
start. (*The couples go back rear and come forward
again.*) Remember your carriage. The carriage is all-
important. (*Assuming an academic manner.*) Let
me explain. To walk well, you must bear yourself
erect, but without stiffness, you must advance both
legs in a straight line, inclining neither to the right
nor the left of your axis; the entire body must par-
ticipate imperceptibly in the general movement.

The COURTIERS *apply themselves.*

CHRISTOPHE (*quietly at first, then with mounting anima-
tion*):   It's a lofty idea, gentlemen, and I'm glad to
see that you have fully understood it, that you have
grasped its profound earnestness.
These new names, these titles of nobility, this
Coronation!
In the past they stole our names
Our pride
Our nobility.
They, I repeat, they stole them.
Pierre, Paul, Jacques, Toussaint. Those are the hu-
miliating brand marks with which they obliterated
our real names.
I myself
your king
can you sense a man's hurt at not knowing the
name he's called by, or to what his name calls him?
Only our Mother Africa knows.

Vehement.

Since we can't rescue our names from the past, we'll
take them from the future.

Tender and Passionate.

With names of glory I will cover your slave names

With names of pride our names of infamy
With names of redemption our orphans' names.
Names of rebirth, gentlemen.

Contemplates the royal ornaments and steps for-
ward. HUGONIN *goes up to him, throws the royal*
mantle around his shoulders, and kneels down to
arrange the folds.

Playthings, rattles, no doubt.
But thunder too.
Thousands of half-naked blacks
vomited up by the sea one night.
Come from God knows where. With their scent of
hunted game.
Thunder: mystic white savannah, as my Bambara
ancestors said.
Thunder: power to speak, to make, to construct, to
build, to be, to name, to bind, to remake. I'll take
them, I know their weight, I'll bear them.

The lights go out. When they go on again, the
Cathedral of Cap Haitien.

SCENE FOUR

~~~~~~

The Coronation. The KING *and* QUEEN *are each kneeling at a prie-dieu.* CORNEILLE BRELLE *and a* DEACON.

CORNEILLE BRELLE (*the Archbishop, officiating*): Profiterisne carissime in Christo Fili et promittis coram Deo et angelis eius deinceps legem justitiam et pacem, Ecclesiaeque Dei populoque tibi subjecto facere ac servare . . . ac invigilare ut pontificibus Ecclesiae Dei condignus et canonicus honos exhibeatur?

The DEACON *holds out the Gospels, which* CHRISTOPHE *kisses. The* ARCHBISHOP *prepares to place the crown on his head.* CHRISTOPHE *snatches it out of his hands and crowns himself.*

CHRISTOPHE: Profiteor.

THE PRESIDENT OF THE COUNCIL OF STATE: Excellency, by the grace of God and the constitutional law of the State, we proclaim you Henry I, sovereign of the islands of La Tortue, Gonave, and other adjacent islands. Destroyer of tyranny, regenerator and benefactor of the Haitian nation, first crowned monarch of the New World.

THE CROWD: Long live Henry. Henry, live forever.

CHRISTOPHE (*standing, holding out his hand before the Gospels*): I swear to preserve the integrity of the territory and the independence of the kingdom; under no pretext to suffer a return to slavery or any measure prejudicial to the freedom or to the civil and political rights of the Haitian people, to govern with a sole view to the interests, the happiness, and the glory of the great Haitian family of which I am the head.

THE MASTER-AT-ARMS: His great and most serene Highness Henry King of Haiti is crowned and enthroned. May he live forever!

The ARCHBISHOP *exits followed by the* DEACON.

THE CROWD: Long live Henry! Henry, live forever!

CHORUS (*singing*):

> Henry, valiant warrior
> Open the gates of victory!
> Henry, valiant, valiant warrior!
> Henry!

Half-darkness. All go out except CHRISTOPHE *who comes forward.*

CHRISTOPHE:

> Ah, oh
> Sprung from the lowest groveling
> From inert suffering
> Sun of sudden rising
> Jewel inestimable,
> I set you
> On the head of this accursed people
> Staff of command
> I clench the fist
> Of my race, yesterday enslaved!
> I clench! Our fists!

SCENE FIVE

Battlefield. Night is falling. Three or four bodies on the stage. One is METELLUS, *who rises to his knees when* MAGNY *enters and draws a dagger.*

GENERAL MAGNY: Didn't I tell you to finish off the wounded?

OFFICER (*enters from the wings. Takes up his position rear, his rifle aimed at* METELLUS): This one, sir, is the chief of the rebels. I felt bound to consult you.

MAGNY: Very well. You are Metellus, the rebel leader?

METELLUS: I am.

MAGNY: Why this uprising? What is your grievance against Christophe? Speak.

METELLUS (*on his knees, rises to his feet in the course of the speech*):

Driven by the cruel whip of a dream
I stumbled from stone to stone
down, down to your threshold, Death
and summoned you.
I've been in Bédoret, in Serpent Gulch, Pierrot's
    Ridge
Pleasance, in places where it wasn't pleasant to be:
Pierced to the bone with rain
brambles, fever, fear
hungry
sleeping with open eyes in the morning dew
in the stillness of night.

I've known flight and terror, fighting
in the days when we took faith by the throat
with Toussaint!
Good fighting blood flowed in our veins.
On the wild mountain trails, on the steep slopes
of the gorges
amid the barking of the guns
we saw Hope
(the palms of her maiden hands glistened
in the night of her skin like the gold in the hollows of
        the dark leaves of the caïmito tree)
we saw her
we (our pus dried by the red coral leaf)
saw her dancing
        with her inexorable bare breasts
        and her unfaltering blood
(She was the Madwoman who harangued
our timid blood
and wouldn't let it rot in ease and glut or pittance)
Rich raucous blood it was
and bitter manioc without bandage covered our
        wounds!
Damnation!
        We were going to build a country
                all of us together!
Not just to stake out this island!
A country open to all the islands!
To black men everywhere. The blacks of the whole
        world.
But then came politicoes
cutting the house in two
laying hands on our mother
disfiguring her in the eyes of the world
making her into a crude pitiful puppet.
Christophe! Pétion!
Double tyranny, I reject them both

the brute
the haughty skeptic—
Who can say which is the most malignant.
High promise!
To salute you with a man's salute
we watched on the crests
and deep down in the gorges. We watched
with our faces to this black soil, reddening it
with our fertile blood, obedient to the commands
and fears of the imperious conch.
Now, O death

He unbuckles his cartridge belt and throws it away.

let me fall like an incomparable dream.
I won't thank you for a respite.

MAGNY (*to the* OFFICER):   Go ahead. Grant the poor
man's wish. Put him out of his misery.

The OFFICER *fires—*METELLUS *dies. Darkness. The
other corpses are removed. Battle sounds.* METELLUS
*remains. A sound of trumpets. Soldiers come in with
flags, followed by* CHRISTOPHE, VASTEY, MAGNY, *and*
HUGONIN. CHRISTOPHE *kneels down and speaks while
looking at the body.* HUGONIN *walks around the body
and looks to see what the King is doing.*

CHRISTOPHE: It's been a hard day. Many men have
fallen. And wide reaches of this country, our country, have been lost, alas, alas, poor face that our
nails have scraped too deep. Drouillard, Garesche,
Deschezelles, too boldly scarred, good soil, harvests
never reaped, a chunk of holy bread from our good
Haitian earth, and now look: wells overgrown with
briars, charred shattered walls deep in wild banana
thickets, cactuses thrusting out their swords. Dry
wave of thornbush. And the stench! Do you smell it?
I'm not a sailor, but this is what Haiti must be to

the discoverer's nostrils: this smell of dried blood that rasps your throat, this smell of sickening mold, this smell of a holocaust unwelcome to the gods. Luckily the end is in sight. Tomorrow it will all be over.

A soldier enters carrying a two-cornered hat on the end of his rifle. CHRISTOPHE *laughs, followed by the others.*

Hm, looks as if Pétion didn't have time to pick up his hat. We'll return it tomorrow.

He sings:

> Grenadier go charging
> Them that have died, too bad, too bad
> Them that have died, too bad, too bad
> Got no mama
> Got no papa
> Them that have died—too bad, too bad.

The OFFICERS *laugh. The* SOLDIERS *cry hurrah. Trumpets. All exit except* CHRISTOPHE *and* VASTEY. CHRISTOPHE *picks up a handful of dust.*

CHRISTOPHE:

> Look, Vastey, all flat, flat
> dust and rubble
> earth and straw
> crumbling mud walls.
> Stone, that's what I want!
> Cement, give me cement!
> All this, oh! to set it upright!
> Upright in the face of the world, and solid!

Aides come and go.

MAGNY (*enters*):   Sire, forgive me, but we are waiting

for the order to attack and the troops are getting impatient.

CHRISTOPHE: Forget it, Magny.

MAGNY: Never has the situation been more favorable. Pétion is at bay. Take the opportunity.

CHRISTOPHE (with authority): Forget it, I tell you. There will be no attack. I've abandoned the whole campaign. And to begin with, we're not going through with this siege. I've sent an emissary to Pétion. I hope he will realize that the time has come to end our quarrels, to build this country, and to unite our people against a danger that's more pressing than you think, that threatens its very existence.

MAGNY: I can't believe it. Such an understanding is inconceivable. If we don't defeat them, they will defeat us. Forgive me, your Majesty.

CHRISTOPHE: We have to believe it's possible, Magny. Somebody has to take the first step and it may as well be me. I have spoken!

MAGNY: I only hope that your eyes aren't opened too late.

CHRISTOPHE (imperiously): Enough!

Half-darkness. Those present are grouped on the left. When the light goes on, the Senate in Port-au-Prince appears on the right. The senators are sitting in a grandstand.

SCENE SIX

~~~~~~

The Senate.

LEADER OF THE OPPOSITION: My respected colleagues: In view of what we have just heard, I cannot refrain from communicating my dire misgivings to the Assembly. Yes, gentlemen, there is one thing of which I am sure, of which we are all sure, to wit, that Christophe's monarchy is a caricature. But I am beginning to wonder whether we ourselves cut a better figure, whether this Republic of ours is not a caricature of a republic and our Parliament a caricature of a parliament. Mr. President, this you must know: the Assembly has a right to be informed, and it is your duty to keep us informed. Why these circumlocutions? Why this secretiveness? What is being plotted? What machinations are going on behind the nation's back?

PÉTION: I accept the battle on the ground which the opposition (for we are proud to tolerate an opposition) has ill-advisedly chosen. I have no intention of hiding anything from the Assembly or of unduly influencing your free decision. I am a democrat; it is my desire to be not the commander, but the guide of a free nation. Accordingly, I will conceal nothing from the nation. The nation will decide, and when the nation has decided, rest assured, Pétion will act.

LEADER OF THE OPPOSITION: Then speak! Speak! Explain yourself. What does General Christophe really want? What is he demanding? That we recognize him as our leader? And on what does he base his claim? On all the innocent blood he has shed?

Applause.

PÉTION: If the opposition (and it is our title to glory that we tolerate an opposition), if the opposition had been guided less by a spirit of precipitation and perverse distrust than by the moderation, the circumspection, the probity which should at all times inspire the parliament of a free republic, then no one, to the joy of our enemies, would have troubled this hour of national unanimity with a vain quarrel. Indeed, Christophe proposes the reunification of the island. It goes without saying that the island would be unified under his authority, his Royal Munificence deigning, I presume, to honor you and me with the small change of a few subordinate offices, the sop of a sinecure or two. In short, we should become the subjects of his Most Christophian Majesty!

A DEPUTY: It's an outrage.

A DEPUTY: No compromise with the tyrant.

A DEPUTY: He's a pompous pasha.

A DEPUTY: Rather Louis XVIII than Christophe!

A DEPUTY: We call down the wrath of heaven on his head.

The lights go out.

SCENE SEVEN

~~~~~~

The Senate disappears. CHRISTOPHE, VASTEY, MAGNY *still on the battlefield.* OFFICERS *and* AIDES *enter.*

MAGNY: Well, Sire, now we know what's what.

CHRISTOPHE: Poor Africa! Poor Haiti, I mean. Anyway, it's the same thing. There: tribes, languages, rivers, castes, the jungle, village against village. Here: blacks, mulattoes, quadroons, witch doctors, and heaven knows what else, clans, castes, shades of color, distrust and competition, cock fights, dogs fighting over bones, flea fights! (*Roaring.*) Dust! Dust! All dust. No stone. Dust! Shit and dust! (*Calmly.*) All right, Magny, give the troops their marching orders. To the Cape! To the north!

MAGNY: To the Cape?

CHRISTOPHE: Yes, to the Cape. Forward, march.

HUGONIN (*playing the gadfly*):   Here we go, comrades! We're changing our course. With or without lunch, we're off to the Cape. The King has spoken: we're fighting fleas. (*Singing softly*):

> A louse and a flea
> On a dressmaker's dummy
> Arguing
> While playing rummy
>
> The louse was mad
> So was the flea

You lousy louse
Leggo of me.

CHRISTOPHE: Is this a time to be singing, Hugonin?
(*To* VASTEY.) There you have it, Vastey. The human material needs recasting. How are we going to do it? I don't know. We'll start on a small scale. In our little workshop. The smallest country in the world is enormous if the hand is big and the will unflagging . . . And now, forward march! (*They go out. Fanfares.*)

SCENE EIGHT

~~~~~~

Christophe's villa. A banquet to celebrate the first anniversary of the coronation. CHRISTOPHE *and his court,* VASTEY, HUGONIN, MAGNY, CHANLATTE, *and* LADIES. *During the whole scene* CHANLATTE *sits apart, writing, inspired and self-satisfied.*

CHRISTOPHE (*relaxed*): I've heard that in France the banquet is held the same day as the coronation.

MASTER OF CEREMONIES: Yes, your Majesty. (*Taking a high-sounding academic tone*): In Rheims, in the great hall of the Archbishop's palace, in the presence of all the King's dignitaries, the Royal Steward brings in His Majesty's padlock.

CHRISTOPHE: His padlock? That's a funny thing.

MASTER OF CEREMONIES: Actually it's a coffer; the Royal Cupbearer bears the saucer.

HUGONIN: The saucer, you say?

MASTER OF CEREMONIES: His Majesty's saucer, glasses, and decanter; the Royal Meat Carver bears His Majesty's ladle and carving knife. All present are clad in robes and mantles of black velvet lined with gold ... I might add that a dais has been set up for the Queen and the Princesses ...

CHRISTOPHE: Strange! Oh well, we may not have a queen, but at least we have Madame Christophe, not up on a platform, but right here beside us, which is better. Tradition be damned. Today my Royal

Cupbearer won't pour any wine, my Royal Meat Carver won't carve a blessed thing.

HUGONIN (*crawling on all fours*): Majesty, your words break my heart and carve my gizzard. (*Singing softly.*)

> This one plucks it
> This one cooks it
> This one eats it all
> There's nothing left for the little fellow
> Lick the platter, friend
> Lick the platter ...

CHRISTOPHE: Don't worry, gentlemen. You won't serve, you'll be waited on.

HUGONIN: I'm glad to hear that. Now I can breathe again. You've given me back my life, your Majesty. My life and my appetite.

CHANLATTE (*the official poet, declaiming*):

Oh sweet reeds ripening in the yellow plain!

CHRISTOPHE: What's the trouble, Chanlatte? Why that sniveling, why those plaintive sighs in the midst of this joyous banquet?

CHANLATTE: Nothing at all, your Majesty. Just a poem to the glory of rum, considered as a national beverage.

CHRISTOPHE: National? National beverage? That's very interesting. Let's hear it.

CHANLATTE:

> Oh sweet reeds ripening in the yellow plain!
> Far off I hear a hundred presses sigh
> Crushing the nectar from the knotted cane
> Transformed to sugar, it glitters to the eye
> Or trickling golden from the spigot hole
> It bubbles up and overflows the bowl.

CHRISTOPHE: That's rum all right. Splendid, Chanlatte.
It sounds very patriotic. We'll have it taught in the
schools.

HUGONIN (*still on all fours, crawls to the King*):   What
is this? No more beer? No more champagne? I'm
as patriotic and anti-white as the next man, but I
won't deny that champagne . . .

CHRISTOPHE: Damnation! Yes or no, do we or don't
we need our own national poetry? To hell with
champagne. You guzzler, you! Here, catch, to con-
sole you for the champagne. Enjoy yourself. (*He
tosses him a mouthful of something.*) Ah! Why,
there's Prézeau! What's up? A message?

PRÉZEAU (*enters with a tray*):   A message, your Majesty. A letter from London, brought by Sir Alexis
Popham.

CHRISTOPHE (*opening the letter*):   Ah, it's from Wilberforce, my noble friend! Best wishes for the anniversary of my coronation! . . . (*All the* COURTIERS *ap-
plaud.*) Ha! He writes that he has had me enrolled
in several scientific societies, not to mention the
British Bible Society. (CHRISTOPHE *rises and goes to
the* ARCHBISHOP. *General laughter.*) What do you
think of that, Archbishop? It can't do any harm. But
see here, Wilberforce, you're not telling me anything
new, I've heard all that before. (*Reading.*) Bah!
You don't invent a tree, you plant it. You don't ex-
tract the fruit, you let it grow. A nation isn't a sud-
den creation, it's a slow ripening, year after year,
ring after ring. Ha, that's a good one! Sow the seeds
of civilization, he says. Yes, unfortunately, it grows
slowly.

Damnation!

Let time do its work.

Time, time! But how can we wait when time is
holding a knife to our throats? How can we wait for

the sun, the rain, the seasons when the fate of a
people is at stake? Ridiculous!

MADAME CHRISTOPHE: Christophe! Christophe!
I'm only a poor woman. I
was a servant, I the Queen
at the Sign of the Crown.
A crown on my head won't make me
anything more than a plain woman
a good black wife who says to her husband:
Take care, Christophe!
If you try to put the roof of one hut on another
it will be too little or too big!
Christophe, don't ask too much of people or of
   yourself.
Besides, I'm a mother.
And when I see you carried away by the wild horse
   of your heart
my own heart
stumbles, and I say to myself:
if only the day doesn't come when the misery of the
   children
tells the story of a father's immoderation.
Our children, Christophe, think of our children.
Oh God, how will it end?

CHRISTOPHE: I ask too much of men? But not enough
of black men, Madame. If there's one thing that
riles me as much as slaveholders' talk, it's to hear
our philanthropists proclaim, with the best of inten-
tions of course, that all men are men and that there
are neither whites nor blacks. That's thinking in an
armchair, not in the world. All men have the same
rights? Agreed. But some men have more duties
than others. That's where the inequality comes in.
In the challenge. Does anyone believe that all
men, all I say, without privilege, without special
exemption, have known capture, deportation, slav-

ery, collective reduction to the level of animals, the
monstrous insult, the total outrage that we have
suffered, the all-denying spittle plastered on our bodies, spat into our faces. We alone, Madame, do you
hear me, we blacks. From the bottom of the pit we
cry out, from the bottom of the pit we cry out for
air, light, the sun. And if we're going to climb out,
don't you see that we need tense muscles, clenched
teeth, and cool clear heads—ah yes, heads! And
that's why I have to ask more of blacks than of
other people, more faith, more enthusiasm, a step,
another step, and still another, and never a step
backward.

MADAME CHRISTOPHE: A king, yes, you're a king.
Do you know, Christophe, how I see a king in my
little kinky head?
All right, I'll tell you. In the middle of the savannah
ravaged by a malignant sun, the great mombin tree
    with
its dense round leaves, under which the cattle
    thirsting
for shade take refuge.
But you? You?
Sometimes I wonder
if you, taking everything into your hands
trying to manage everything
if you're not the big fig tree
that grabs hold of all the vegetation around it
and stifles it.

CHRISTOPHE:
It's called the "cursed fig tree."
Watch your tongue, woman.

With a start.

Listen. Somewhere in the night the tom-tom's beat-
    ing . . .

Somewhere in the night my people are dancing . . .
    Every day
they dance . . . and every night . . . the ocelot's in
    the bush,
the prowler is at our doors, the manhunter is lurking
    in
wait with his gun, his net, his muzzle; the trap is
ready to be sprung, our persecutors are dogging our
    heels,
and my people dance!

Imploring.

But who
who
will offer me
something more than a priest's litany, more than
    versified praises
more than a parasite's patter or a wife's precautions?
Something that will put this people to work
Something that will educate, no, that will train this
    people?
That reminds me, Prézeau, send me Martial Besse.
And you, you lazy tipplers, what are you waiting
for? Go join the dance! Clear out, clear out, I said.

The COURTIERS *leave in small groups. Only* HUGONIN
and the QUEEN *remain.*

What do I want with women and priests and cour-
    tiers!

To HUGONIN.

Don't you hear me? Clear out, I say. I'm the King,
I'll keep watch by myself.

HUGONIN *takes the Queen's arm and leads her out.*

BESSE (*enters. He is a young European engineer*):   Here
I am, your Majesty.

CHRISTOPHE: Ah, it's you, Martial Besse, the engineer,
the builder.
That's a good trade. That's what I want to be,
the builder of this people.
Well, Martial, haven't you anything to say?
An idea? A suggestion?

MARTIAL BESSE: Majesty, to build up a patrimony for a
people, its own patrimony of beauty, of power, of
assurance! What task could be more worthy of a
paraclete, of the man who calls a people to its out-
ermost limits, who awakens them to their hidden
powers.

CHRISTOPHE: Thank you, Martial Besse . . . Thank you
. . . Your idea is good: a patrimony. Except that I
should speak of a patrimony of energy and pride.
Yes, pride, why not? Look at the swelling chest of
the earth, the earth stretching and tensing its loins
as it shakes off sleep, the first step out of chaos, the
first step to heaven.

MARTIAL BESSE: Majesty. These are terrifying slopes to
build on.

CHRISTOPHE: Exactly. This people has to want, to gain,
to achieve something. Against fate, against history,
against nature. That's it. Extravagant venture of our
bare hands! Insane challenge of our wounded hands!
On this mountain a solid cornerstone, a firm foundation. Assault of heaven or sun's resting place, I do
not know—fresh troops charging in the morning.
Look, Besse. Imagine on this very unusual platform,
turned toward the north magnetic pole, walls one
hundred and thirty feet high and thirty feet thick,
lime and bagasse, lime and bull's blood, a citadel.
No, not a palace. Not a fortress to guard my property. No, the citadel, the freedom, of a whole people. Built by the whole people, men and women,
young and old, and for the whole people. Look, its

head is in the clouds, its feet dig into the valleys. It's a city, a fortress, a battleship of stone. Impregnable, Besse, impregnable. Yes, Mr. Engineer, to every people its monuments. This people, forced to its knees, needed a monument to make it stand up. There it is. Risen! A watchtower! (*Spellbound.*)

Look! . . . No, look! It's alive. Sounding its horn in the fog. Lighting up in the night. Canceling out the slave ship. Charging over the waves. My friends, the acrid salt we drank and the black wine of the sand, I, we, we who were flung ashore by the surf, I have seen the enigmatic prow, spewing blood and foam, plowing through the sea of shame.

Let my people, my black people, salute the tide smell of the future.

A vision of the Citadel stands out, illumined, against a double chain of mountains.

Act II

SCENE ONE

~~~~~~

A field in the Haitian countryside. Five or six PEASANTS
taking a rest. A voice off-stage singing:

> Poor prisoner, oh!
> Slaves at the mill
> Slaving for Robertine
> My lady wife.
> Sho, sho, Dhalia.

FIRST PEASANT: Hey, this water's cool! It comes from
the river that flows between the pink apple trees.

SECOND PEASANT: I won't say different. It's cool, but a
slug of rum isn't bad either. There's nothing like a
slug of rum to rest a body bathed in sweat. There's
no better pick-me-up.

FIRST PEASANT: It's going to rain. And not rum. Look,
Bédoret Hill is smoking, and when Bédoret smokes,
it means bad weather. It never fails. All the same,
it's mighty nice country, coffee trees, cacao trees,
and this water that flows through the pink apple
trees and the bamboo.

SECOND PEASANT (*stands up*):   I won't say different,
friend. The country's all right, but the times are
bad.

FIRST PEASANT: That's no way to talk. Times are neither good nor bad. Taste is in the mouth. It's the
way you take things that makes them good or bad.

SECOND PEASANT: That's right, friend. But the best way

to take bad times is in bed. And certain people won't let you. They shove the times down your throat like medicine.

FIRST PEASANT: There's nothing wrong with good herb medicine that builds you up.

SECOND PEASANT (*standing up*):   No, there's nothing wrong with good herb medicine. But here's what I've been saying to myself: when we threw the whites into the sea, it was to have this land for ourselves, not to slave for other people, even if they're as black as we are, but to have the land for ourselves like a wife.

FIRST PEASANT: Don't get rebellious. . . . Maybe Christophe is a little free with the big stick. But that doesn't prevent him from being a good father and a good husband. Hm! If you ask me, Pétion's too soft, he lets things go to seed. He's like a mother who spoils her boy behind the father's back. But a father's a father; when he's hard, it's for the son's own good and because he's proud of his son. Think it over, friend, think it over.

SECOND PEASANT: I've thought it over. And what we need isn't pride, it's good sense.

FIRST PEASANT: God is good, friend. Best thing we can do is trust Him.

SECOND PEASANT: Sure He's good, but awful high up. The hard part is getting your prayers to climb. Mercy me, with those damned Royal Dahomeys around, we can't even get up a little Voodoo meeting. The second the drum begins to beat, there they come, cloppety-clop, cloppety-clop. Looks like there's no more freedom for the gods than for people.

FIRST PEASANT: Now, now, friend. Take it easy . . .

Sound of a drum.

A DRUMMER *in uniform enters and marches around*

the stage drumming. The PEASANTS *stand up and form ranks.*

DRUMMER: A proclamation from King Christophe: In view of the gross abuses and malfeasances that have been reported among the farm population, I hereby most urgently proclaim:

Article 1: All overseers and farm workers are under obligation to perform their duties with the same exactitude, obedience, and willingness as the members of the armed forces.

Article 2: All overseers and farm workers who do not scrupulously perform their agricultural duties will be apprehended and punished with the same severity as soldiers who fall short of their duties.

Article 3: The generals and high-ranking officers of the armed forces are hereby instructed to enforce the present order, for the execution of which I hold them personally responsible. I trust that their effort in behalf of the public welfare will be untiring, sustained by the conviction that freedom cannot endure without labor.

signed Christophe

SCENE TWO

~~~~~~~~~~~~~~~~~~~~~~~~~~~~~~~~

In the palace, CHRISTOPHE *alone.*

PRÉZEAU (*enters*):   Your Highness, Archbishop Brelle, Duke of the Cove, is here.

CHRISTOPHE: Good. Show him in. (PRÉZEAU *exits and returns with* BRELLE.) I have sent for you, Archbishop, to tell you that your request for repatriation to France is not very much to my liking. I made you Duke of the Cove; I built you the finest episcopal palace in the New World, and now you wish to abandon me.

ARCHBISHOP: Your Majesty, after twenty years in the tropics I am entitled to a rest.

CHRISTOPHE: Rest! Rest! That's all they can think of! Even you, Brelle, my good friend.

ARCHBISHOP: There's my aged mother in France, Your Majesty.

CHRISTOPHE: There's still so much to be done, Brelle!

ARCHBISHOP: Your throne is secure, the kingdom is prospering, and I am only an old priest exhausted by his evangelical labors.

CHRISTOPHE: Good Lord, Brelle. When you've embarked on a great task, you don't drop it, not even to comfort your aged mother . . .
Never mind! I'll think about it.

BRELLE *exits.* CHRISTOPHE, *angrily.*

False words
False lips
Double tongues
And double hearts.
Supple necks!
Men? . . . Bah! . . . Shadows.
My court is a theater of shadows.
But I read on the blackboard everything that's
written under their thick skulls!

SCENE THREE

At Cape Henry, a drawing room. Two upper-class LADIES.

FIRST LADY: My dear, have you heard the latest? It's a
scream, and it concerns our sex . . . Imagine, he's
mobilized the royal family . . . even the girls.
Athenais and Amethyst—the princesses, as we call
them—have to show themselves on the building
sites at least once a week.

SECOND LADY: And what for, may I ask? To sell drinks?

FIRST LADY: You'll never guess. One is supposed to
wave a flag and the other is expected to sing to
revive the drooping spirits of the workmen. They've
even thought up titles for them. Queen of the Flag
and Queen Songbird. Well, what do you think of it?

SECOND LADY: I think it's dreadful. Simply dreadful.
But here's Baron Vastey. Good morning, my Lord,
and welcome!

Enter VASTEY. ISABELLE, *a young servant girl, enters
from the other side, takes his coat and exits.*

VASTEY: Madame, I kiss your hand!

SECOND LADY: I'm so glad to see you, Monsieur Vastey.
You've become quite a stranger now that you've
taken on the burdens of the State.

VASTEY: Let's try not to think about that, Madame.

SECOND LADY: We can't help thinking about it. Once

upon a time there was a king, full of the wildest ideas. And his subjects wondered . . .

VASTEY: No, they contemplated the rare, the magnificent spectacle of a great force at work, excessive perhaps, but still a force, Madame.

FIRST LADY: A force? Gracious, I hadn't thought of that. A force? But what of us? Such a force can only crush us.

VASTEY: For my part, Madame, I expect it to exalt us, and first of all in our own eyes.

SECOND LADY: Meanwhile, it bears a terrifying resemblance to something we all knew very well in the past, something against which you, Monsieur Vastey, and I honor you for it, took up arms. In the past.

VASTEY (shrugging his shoulders):   Sometimes history offers only one path. And all are obliged to take it.

FIRST LADY: Then the paths of freedom and of slavery are identical?

SECOND LADY: What a delightful paradox! Do you mean that King Christophe employs the means of slavery to attain the ends of freedom?

VASTEY: But have you considered that the Devil's money, well spent, might be equivalent to God's money? My God, Madame, is the grandeur of the State and freedom for black men.

FIRST LADY: I can see, Monsieur Vastey, that I shall never get the better of a lawyer like you. Let's forget about politics. Isabelle, come play the harpsichord. (ISABELLE enters.) The child has a delightful voice. Isabelle, sing us that charming ballad about Ooreka.

VASTEY: Ooreka?

FIRST LADY: She's the heroine of a novel that has all Paris in tears . . . The story of a little black girl brought up in a white family in Europe. She is unhappy about her color and dies of her unhappiness.

VASTEY: Ah! That's interesting. Very interesting.

ISABELLE (*singing*):

> A daughter of black Africa
> Flower of burning distant skies
> Ooreka, poor unhappy child
> Bewailed her lot with bitter sighs.
>
> O France, O country of my dreams
> Land where I always longed to stay
> How could I know that on your shores
> I'd be unloved from day to day.
>
> My soul was worthy to be white
> As angels in the sky so free.
> Almighty God, what thanks I'd sing
> If you had just done that for me.
>
> But no, you made me to be scorned.
> And now Ooreka's life is done.
> But death is sweet for one like me
> Who ne'er was loved by anyone.

FIRST LADY: Bravo! Bravo! It's heartbreaking. What do you think of it, Monsieur Vastey?

VASTEY: It makes me think of Christophe, Madame. Do you know why he labors day and night? Do you know the purpose behind his "wild ideas," as you call them, and his frantic efforts? He's fighting for the day when no little black girl, anywhere in the world, will be ashamed of her skin, when no little black girl's color will stand in the way of her dreams.

SCENE FOUR

~~~~~~

A terrace outside the palace. To one side a telescope is set up. VASTEY *sitting at a table writing.* CHRISTOPHE *pacing in agitation.* HUGONIN, *sitting on a stool, helps* VASTEY, *picking up papers that fall and examining documents with a knowing air.* BRELLE *in a corner, reading his breviary.*

CHRISTOPHE: The citadel isn't getting ahead fast enough. We've got to work harder, put everybody to work, yes, everybody, the women and children too.

VASTEY: Children?

CHRISTOPHE: Yes, damn it, children. It's their future that we're building. The rampart that will prevent the hawk from swooping down on its game! The support for the frail young tree. And that means everybody has to work. Labor service, carrying stones. Every woman ten stones a day. It won't kill them. A child can tote from two to five, according to his age. Where's Prézeau?

PRÉZEAU (*entering*): Here, your Majesty.

CHRISTOPHE (*speaks with mounting anger. During this speech* HUGONIN *stands beside the king, taking a lively interest*): Prézeau, I want you to attend to Bazin. I made him Count of Redstone, I gave him Deschapelles as his estate, and now I hear he's having the peasants flogged. Damnation! I gave him workmen, not slaves. Send a platoon of the Royal Dahomeys. Have the foreman in charge of the flogging tied to a tree on the public square. Assemble the people. And see to it that he's cut to pieces with a saber. As for Bazin, I want him to report here tomorrow. We can't have too many hands working on the Citadel.

Oh yes! . . . and you'll say a word, a strong word, mind you, to the master of the corral at Bronze Pasture. Tell Joker Socrates—yes, that's his name— that I'm in no joking mood . . . He's written that one of my English stallions is dead. Tell him once and for all that Socrates is a man and therefore mortal. But that my horses aren't men. They may change their coats, but they don't die . . . I give him three days to replace my horse . . . Or I'll have him sliced in two.

It's time to teach those niggers a lesson who think the Revolution means taking the place of white men and behaving the same way.—Oh yes, Hugonin. I'm putting you in charge of public morality.

HUGONIN: Public morality?

CHRISTOPHE: That's right.

HUGONIN: Oh, thank you, Your Majesty. Coming from my Prince, nothing could touch me so deeply as such an homage to my character, my morals, my virtue, my . . .

CHRISTOPHE: Never mind that. All reports indicate that the institution of marriage is in a bad way in our country. Our people have stopped getting married. They just shack up . . . By the way, are the peasants here? Bring the scoundrels in. (PEASANTS and PEAS-ANT WOMEN enter. Men and women form separate groups.) Well, gentlemen, I've been hearing fine things about you.

HUGONIN: Yes, Your Majesty. They go chasing around

without rhyme or reason . . . They're fornicators, your Majesty. Fornicators! It's shocking.

CHRISTOPHE: I see! You might as well say conspirators. (*All the* PEASANTS *laugh.*) Well, this has got to stop. (PEASANTS *are frightened and grow solemn.*) Our State needs a solid foundation; when I say foundation, I mean the family; and that means women with permanent husbands. I won't have my subjects running around with their flies open like savages. It is therefore my decision that you will all get married—immediately!

HUGONIN: Yes, ladies and gentlemen, the King in his paternal solicitude and I as Minister of Public Morality have decided to save you the trouble of looking around . . . You are all here, my sons and daughters, I'm glad to see you. There's a mate here for every one of you, and vice versa. (*Picks a man and a woman and leads them together. The couple steps forward, passes in front of* BRELLE, *who has come front stage and now blesses them. Then the couple goes to a corner and waits. The scene is several times repeated in the course of* HUGONIN'S *speech. The couples gather in the corner.*) What do you say, boy? How's this little lady appeal to you? Not bad, eh? Too fat? Never mind that, fat women are the best . . . Going, going . . . she's yours! . . . You want the little skinny one? Done . . . We've got something for every taste . . You over there! You're built like Hercules in person . . . And look at the croup, the muscles on that young lady! I bet she could throw an elephant. Well, what are you waiting for . . . Help yourselves, gentlemen. We've a shoe for every foot. Your Majesty, a woman like that is a blessing. She'll give us a whole work gang before she's through. Let's go, ladies and gentlemen, our agriculture needs strong arms and the State needs soldiers . . . Well, good night, ladies and gentlemen, and the State expects you all to do your duty. (*The* PEASANTS *go out with dignity.*)

CHRISTOPHE: Go to it, Brelle! I bet it's the biggest wedding of your career.

HUGONIN (*singing*):

> Marry me young, marry me young
> 'Cause corn picked too late
> Is scrawny
> Corn picked too late
> Is scrawny.

MAGNY and RICHARD *are brought in.*

CHRISTOPHE: All right, Hugonin, that will do. Well, that's settled. And now, gentlemen! I am extremely displeased with you. Things have come to a pretty pass. The kingdom is threatened with indiscipline, anarchy. Yes, gentlemen, anarchy! I am obliged to take action . . . Prézeau! Escort Magny to the Citadel . . . As for you, Richard, you will leave for Thomasico this afternoon with the rank of captain. (*He tears off Richard's insignia*).

MAGNY and RICHARD: To the Citadel? . . . Thomasico? Captain?

CHRISTOPHE: Exactly, gentlemen! . . . Tell me, Pleasance, how many steps has our royal stairway of Sans-Souci?

MAGNY: I never stopped to count them. But I can tell you one thing: they're mighty steep and narrow.

CHRISTOPHE: Well, I've counted them for you. There are sixty-four of them. And yesterday I saw you, in contempt of all dignity, climbing them four at a time! What a spectacle! A Duke climbing the stairway of his King's palace four at a time!

MAGNY: But . . .

CHRISTOPHE: But me no buts. Just remember the dictates of etiquette, the duties incumbent on your rank, the demands of the State. Fit him out with silk stockings, Prézeau. You catch my meaning? The French call them chains. That will slow him down. That will show him how to climb the steps of Sans-Souci. Dismissed! . . . As for you, Richard, since you oblige me to explain, your conduct at last night's ball was ridiculous. I will not have my nobles playing the clown. At my court, sir, one does not dance the bamboola.

RICHARD: But Your Majesty! That filthy hole at the ends of the kingdom?

CHRISTOPHE: Exactly. It's just the place for you. You'll be able to dance to your heart's content . . . Dismissed!

HUGONIN (*escorts them out, singing*):

> The Emperor was dere,
> dancing bimbo, boola.

CHRISTOPHE: Shut up, Hugonin! Ah, what a trade! Training this people. Like a schoolmaster shaking his ruler at a nation of dunces! Gentlemen, I trust you understand the significance of these punishments. Either we smash everything, or we put the country on its feet. Smash—it's conceivable . . . A country razed to the ground, naked nakedness. Why not? That would be a freedom of sorts. There's still the earth, the sky, the stars, the night, and we blacks with our freedom, our roots, our wild bananas. That's one way of looking at it. Or else we build, and you know what that means. It means bearing burdens, it means climbing higher and higher, further and further. There's a choice. I've made it.

HUGONIN: Majesty, the Council of State is here, and the people, too, burning to harangue you.

VASTEY: I take the liberty of reminding Your Majesty

that the emissary of the King of France is also
waiting; he's been cooling his heels for several hours.

CHRISTOPHE: Never fear! I'll receive him, but in his
turn. First the Council of State. (*He goes to the
telescope while the Council of State, consisting of
four* TOWNSMEN *and one aged* PEASANT, *enter.*)

THE CHAIRMAN OF THE COUNCIL OF STATE: Majesty, the
Council of State is confident of expressing the
sentiment of the whole country in laying before
Your Majesty a tribute of admiration for the un-
paralleled determination with which you have
championed the cause of Haiti and the liberty of its
people . . . (*Turning toward another member of
the Council.*) Am I doing all right?—And now my
colleagues and myself, speaking for all the classes
that make up our harmonious society, cherish the
hope the nation will be rewarded for its long effort
and permitted, in the shadow of your sheltering
arm, to enjoy the repose which its heroic struggle
and unflagging toil have earned.

CHRISTOPHE (*who has returned from the telescope*):
Gentlemen, thank you for coming. I am glad to see
the entire nation gathered here in the persons of its
representatives.

The other members of the Council push the PEASANT
forward.

What I have to tell you concerns the whole nation.
True, the alarms of war are passed, but against the
background of peace our problems and our tasks
only stand out the more urgently. And the prospect
I hold out to you today is not one of leisure. No,
this is no time for resting.

THE PEASANT: Majesty, a canoe may be sea-worthy, but
it doesn't have to fight the tempest day-in day-out;
a ceiba tree can stand up to the wind, but it doesn't

always have to fight the wind . . . Your people are tired.

CHRISTOPHE (*in a burst of rage*): Old man . . . your crown of white hair merits my indulgence. But don't abuse it . . . Frankly, gentlemen, I would curse my victory if to you it meant repose . . .

> Who would awaken your black stone,
> Striking the clear note of men?

I do not release you!

Pointing to the telescope aimed at a sleeping PEASANT.

Gentlemen! Are you aware of the country's situation? . . .
Very well then, take a look! . . . Take a good look.
General Warrior, you look too . . .
Well, what did you see?

FIRST COUNCILOR OF STATE: Uh, uh, a sleeping peasant, your Majesty.

THE PEASANT: A poor tired peasant, your Majesty.

CHRISTOPHE: General Warrior! Battery Twelve in position! Take aim! Fire!

GENERAL WARRIOR: Fire!

HUGONIN: My, oh my! . . . The shanty's blown to smithereens! And the poor bastard . . . hash! Three cheers for the Royal Artillery. Sensitive souls, don't be sad. (*Picks up the telescope and puts it over his shoulders.*) He's gone from the little sleep to the big sleep without even noticing it . . . (*Turns toward* BRELLE *and crosses himself.*) Requiescat in pace! (*Exits with the telescope.*)

CHRISTOPHE: Now you understand. You may go, gentlemen. Wait, just a minute; I said "go," but not like that. Prézeau, to all these big blacks, stout of body and limb, but bloated with eloquence, you will give picks and shovels. Our agriculture has need of arms.

Council of State, forward march! Left, left. (*They go out.*) And now, France, I am ready for you.

(*Enter* VASTEY. *He hands* CHRISTOPHE *Franco de Medina's letter.*

CHRISTOPHE: Good! Bring in Monsieur Franco de Medina!

Two lackeys bring in an armchair for CHRISTOPHE, *who sits down.* FRANCO DE MEDINA, *typical diplomat, is led in.*

(*Very calmly.*) To put it plainly, Monsieur Franco de Medina, what my good cousin the King of France is suggesting is a deal. A deal at the expense of my people. This free people would be enchained again, our glorious army would lay down its arms and submit to the whip, drawing small comfort from the trophies it has amassed on the field of battle. And I, in lackey's braid, would be reduced to lolling around your king's antechambers! . . . (*In a thundering voice.*) All I have to say is this: if you didn't have diplomatic immunity and if this were not a civilized country! . . . Yes, Monsieur, civilized. (*Stands up and strides toward* FRANCO DE MEDINA.)

VASTEY: Permit me, Your Majesty, to remind you of something which cannot have escaped you, to wit, that the ambassador, or better still, the agent of the King of France, is a native of the former Spanish zone of Santo Domingo, now a Spanish province. As such, he is a Haitian before the law and accordingly your Majesty's subject.

CHRISTOPHE (*with a sardonic laugh*):   Right you are. Thank you, Vastey . . . Thank you . . . I see that you were born to understand me and to serve me! Meanwhile, to settle the political question once and for all, kindly inform our cousin France that we are free by right and independent in fact and will never forgo these advantages. No! We will never let anyone overturn the edifice we have built with our hands and cemented with our blood.

FRANCO DE MEDINA: You misunderstand me, Your Majesty. I come with an olive branch.

CHRISTOPHE: Excellent! I can only thank you for reminding me of your existence. Where's Prézeau?

VASTEY: Permit me to remind Your Majesty once again that Monsieur Franco de Medina is a Haitian.

CHRISTOPHE: Prézeau, have the drum sounded. Notify the people! And you, Brelle, you will be needed. He may be a traitor, but his soul is entitled to everlasting peace. That's your province. I wish him to see with his own eyes that we are making provisions for his soul.

HUGONIN *enters, looks at* MEDINA *contemptuously, strips off Medina's fine coat and throws a ragged coat over his shoulders.*

While you are officiating, Monsieur Franco de Medina will stand beside his coffin and listen to his own requiem mass . . . Wait till it's over, Prézeau, and then proceed with care. Gentlemen of his stamp are fastidious. I wouldn't want a single drop of blood to stain his collar. Bon voyage, Monsieur Franco de Medina . . . (*A rolling of drums is heard.* FRANCO DE MEDINA *is led away, impassive, followed by* BRELLE *and* HUGONIN *in procession.*) Prézeau!

PRÉZEAU: Yes, Your Majesty!

CHRISTOPHE: Er. . . It's about Brelle. I made him Archbishop, but his appointment was never confirmed by the Holy See. I have sent a message to the Pope through Péletier in London (who, between you and me, is costing me a pretty penny in sugar and coffee.) But His Holiness doesn't answer. In short,

Brelle's situation is irregular. It's troublesome . . .
extremely troublesome. What do you think,
Prézeau?

PRÉZEAU: It's extremely troublesome, your Majesty.

CHRISTOPHE: It even seems doubtful whether Brelle
is actually an archbishop. What do you say,
Prézeau?

PRÉZEAU: It seems doubtful, your Majesty.

CHRISTOPHE: Bah, that's neither here nor there. My appointment is as good as the Pope's consecration.
What bothers me is that Brelle is getting old.
Moreover, he writes a good deal . . . He talks a good
deal . . . More than the welfare of the State requires.

PRÉZEAU: I await your orders, your Majesty.

CHRISTOPHE: He's an old man, Prézeau, and an old
friend! . . .

PRÉZEAU: He is indeed an old friend, your Majesty.

CHRISTOPHE (cynically):   He talks too much, Prézeau.
He writes too much. But no blood, no blood! A
peaceful death, in his bed . . . He's an old man. So
gently . . . gently . . . But quickly, Prézeau . . .
(More and more vehemently.) Seal up the doors
and windows of his palace! . . . Every last one! . . .
Seal them up! Don't leave anything open, not even
a mouse hole! (PRÉZEAU exits.) Dismissed! (CHRIS-
TOPHE steps forward.) I am giving Brelle the finest
archepiscopal tomb in the New World! . . .

SCENE FIVE

~~~~~~

Near the Archbishop's palace in Cap Haïtien. Groups of passers-by.

THE VOICE OF CORNEILLE BRELLE: Christophe!

A BEGGAR: Did you hear that, friend?

A PASSER-BY: That's from the Archbishop's palace. There are some things it's better not to have heard! (*He runs away.*)

CRY: Christophe!

BEGGAR: Stop that yelling! Looks like some people never had a grandmother. All I remember about my grandmother is the way she ended her little sermons:

> Play wid monkey, yes.
> But leave 'is tail alone.

CRY: Water! Water!

BEGGAR: Still hollering! It makes me thirsty to hear him hollering like that . . . (*Drawing a bottle from his pocket.*) Oops. A little slug of likker. (*Feeling better.*) Say, ain't it a pity, the poor ol' man! Have mercy on him, Mister Satan. Open the door, damn it, let him out. That's the King's confessor in there . . . Wid a big sack of 'is master's sins on his back, not to mention 'is little private bundle, hic-hic, which ain't empty neither. No, no, Satan, it ain't empty . . .

PIERCING SCREAM: Christophe . . . King Christophe!

A WOMAN (*singing a litany*): Virgin Mary, Virgin most helpful, St. Cosmo and St. Damian, Virgin of the Rosary, Virgin of Mercy, Virgin high in grace, Virgin of charity . . .

PIERCING SCREAM: Christophe!

SCENE SIX

~~~~~~

The Citadel: labors suggesting the building of the Pyra-
mids. Men and women working. The men are soldiers
who have been impressed into labor service.

SOLDIER-WORKERS AND WOMEN (*exhausted. Singing*):

> If de master ain't good
> Ol' man God is good!
> Haiti, O Haiti
> Haiti's for all de Haitians.

FIRST SOLDIER-WORKER: I quit! . . . My feet are all
  bloody.

SECOND SOLDIER-WORKER: What about me? My shoulder's coming off.

FIRST WOMAN (*bending over them*): Poor boys! . . .

SECOND WOMAN: You got time to waste, Sal? I ain't
  sorry for no mule niggers.

FIRST WOMAN: You ain't got no heart, gal . . .

SECOND WOMAN (*spitting*): Pooh, pooh! Giddyap . . .
  you mules! Dat's de way to treat 'em. If dey wanna
  ack like mules! . . .

A ROYAL DAHOMEY *appears.*

SOLDIER-WORKERS (*getting reluctantly back to work*):

> If de master ain't good
> Ol' man God is good!
> Haiti, O Haiti
> Haiti's for all de Haitians.

FOREMAN (*enters*):   What is dis? You gonna work or ain't you? I'm telling you for your own good. That's right. Your own good.

SOLDIER-WORKERS (*singing wearily*):

> Poor prisoner, oh!
> Slaves at the mill
> Slaving for Robertine
> My lady wife.
> Shoh, shoh, Dhalia.

> Poor prisoner, oh!
> Slaves at the mill
> Slaving for Robertine
> Already wed.
> Shoh, shoh, Dhalia.

FOREMAN: What is dis? Ain't nobody taking up de chorus? De big man likely to come around any minute. And den, boys, I pity yuh.

SOLDIER-WORKERS (*singing wearily*):

> Oh Dhalia oh!

Enter CHRISTOPHE *with* VASTEY, HUGONIN, *and* GENERAL WARRIOR.

CHRISTOPHE: Well, foreman . . .

FOREMAN: Your Majesty, we can't take it much longer in this weather. Maybe we'd better let the men go home. This wind would take the horns off an ox.

CHRISTOPHE: Bah! Depends on the ox! Look, I'll show you the way an honest black man works.

FOREMAN: You, your Majesty?

CHRISTOPHE: Who'd be the first workman in Haiti if not Christophe? (*He starts working and all revive.*)

FOREMAN: Your Majesty, the trouble is hoisting the cannon up here. The slope is steep and slippery.

I've put a hundred men on the job. They're not getting anywhere.

CHRISTOPHE: Pull fifty of them out. It'll go better.

SOLDIER-WORKERS (*singing*):

> Poor prisoner, oh!
> Slaves at the mill
> The cock goes cock-a-doodle-do
> Back home, back home.
> Shoh, shoh, Dhalia.
>
> Poor prisoner, oh!
> Slaves at the mill
> You'll turn the mill
> Until you die
> Until you die.

CHRISTOPHE (*climbs up on a scaffolding. All look up at him*):   I'm speaking to you as a soldier. Take it from me, it's no fun skedaddling from hill to hill, from bush to bush. That's why I decided to give my people this good stone bulwark, this good stone dog. His face alone will discourage the wolf pack.

HUGONIN: And suppose the French come around anyway? What will they get on their heads? Tomatoes? Mangoes? Pumpkins? Oh no! Good iron cannon balls is what they'll get and a load of Papa Christophe's best grapeshot in their damn white asses!

WORKMEN (*singing*):

> Oh wind, oh wind, oh bring us rain.
> Wind, wind. Oh mother, here's the rain.
> Wind, wind. Oh mother, where were you?
> Oh wind, oh wind, here comes the rain.
> Oh wind, now go and get the pails.
> Oh wind, oh wind, who brings the rain.
> Oh wind, oh wind, the pails are full.
> Oh wind, make fire in the hearth.

Oh wind, oh wind, set cakes to bake.
Oh wind, prepare the manioc.
Oh wind, come help us grate the root.
Oh wind, the cakes are ready baked.
Oh wind, oh wind who brings the rain!
Oh wind, oh wind, oh wind!

A crash of thunder. Lightning. Mounting confusion among the workers.

CHRISTOPHE: What's the matter now? A little lightning? Come along, boys. We've got no time to waste on fireworks. Foreman, give them drums and horns. Let the great horn answer the thunder with cannon, thunder to thunder, face to face. Strike the cymbals. Answer lightning with lightning. Blow the visceral giant conch. We'll answer blind violence with the controlled violence of our lungs.

AIDE-DE-CAMP (*appears*): Your Majesty, lightning has struck the powder stores; the Treasury building is wrecked; the commandant and half the garrison are buried under the ruins.

CHRISTOPHE (*imperious*):
Take heart, boys!
It's just another battle.
Agonglo.
With its saw-tooth leaves gathered around its heart
The pineapple resists.
So the King of Dahomey salutes the future
With his scepter.
Agonglo.

He shakes his sword at the heavens.

Hey, St. Peter, better not make war on us!

Act III

SCENE ONE

~~~~~~

The royal palace. In the background COURTIERS *and*
LADIES *dancing. Front stage,* HUGONIN *and an* OLD MAN
looking on.

OLD MAN: Look . . . Look at that . . . Isn't it wonder-
ful? Doesn't it make you happy to see our own black
men in silk cloaks, with whole forests of feathers on
their hats: blue, red, white . . .

HUGONIN: You've got something there, old timer. It's
better to have them on your head than sticking out
of your ass like our ancestors.

OLD MAN (*excited*):   All you who disparage our race,
our customs, our character, wherever you may be
. . . come right ahead, we're waiting for you . . .

CHANLATTE *enters and listens to the discussion.*

HUGONIN: Don't mind him, he always gets these little
fits of eloquence on great occasions.—Go on,
grandpa, we're listening . . .

OLD MAN (*more and more aroused*):   Say, if you dare,
that we're not worthy of our freedom . . . And you,
philosophers of all countries, who have cast off all
prejudice, who recognize that we too bear the fea-
tures of our common maker. Rejoice to see us living
up to your generous opinions.

HUGONIN: Excellent, grandpa . . . Splendid. What I

71

especially admire is the patriotic way your rum reasons.

CHANLATTE: If you'll permit me to say so, I have expressed similar sentiments in more inspired language. (*Declaiming, glass in hand*):

Ye haughty foe of our triumphant rights
Abjure your errors and renounce your plans.
What can avail the poison of your helpless
Fury against the rock that bears this isle?
Vainly the winds rile up against King Neptune
One glance from him and all the oceans smile.

A propos of plans and poisons, Hugonin, you who are always so well informed, any news of Pétion?

HUGONIN: Boyer, the future president, is well. So well in fact that I wouldn't be surprised if he gave us a little trouble on the border one of these days.

CHANLATTE: What a man! I ask him about Pétion and he tells me about Boyer.

HUGONIN: Well, I trust you've heard of Mademoiselle Jouste, Pétion's mistress. Young Boyer has shown himself a gifted jouster. After dancing attendance on the young lady for some time, he entered the lists boldly. Jousting adroitly, striking not with the edge but with the point, he unsaddled Pétion, who has given up sword play and goes about looking like the Knight of the Mournful Countenance.

And losing his sow
He wept like a cow.

Enter a group including CANDYTOWN, MAGNY, *and* VASTEY, *chatting.*

CANDYTOWN: My word, I'm used to the royal whims, but he's beginning to go too far. Here the Citadel is hardly finished, the people's backs are still aching, and now they're being invited to contribute their

patriotic sweat to the building of a new castle, somewhere near Pierrot's Ridge. And what a castle!
Something out of the Thousand and One Nights.

MAGNY: Thousand and One Days would be more like
it. And long days at that. Yes, it's right here in *The
Gazette*. A palace for a congress of all the sovereigns
of the world who deign to take a little trip to Haiti.

VASTEY: Why not? Delirious clouds overhead, at our
feet the sea foam vomited out by two worlds. That's
where God has put us. Our backs to the Pacific; before us Europe and Africa; on either side, the Ameri-
cas. Why, this extraordinary concretion of ours is
situated at the confluence of all the world's tides, at
the focal point of every ebb and flow. And what a
view it offers on all sides!

MAGNY: My dear Admiral, you haven't a single ship in
your fleet yet, but set your mind at rest: Haiti itself
is a great ship, or to put it more bluntly, one big
galley. And the whole crew has tropic fever.

HUGONIN: Hush! Gag the galley slaves. The King!

Three LADIES *enter. The* COURTIERS *go to the rear.*

FIRST LADY: You're looking lovely, my dear. What an
adorable dress; and that scarf: the color is bewitch-
ing.

SECOND LADY: Thank you for the compliments, but I'm
really not in the mood. I've had such a fright! I
start up the palace staircase, and what do I see, al-
most flapping in my face, but a frizzy—in broad
daylight one of those little night hawks that bring
bad luck! I start to run. I fall down, I pick myself
up. The others did the same. It was a panic, one of
the sentries even let his gun go off.

THIRD LADY: When such things happen, I always say a
prayer, it helps me every time. Three times in a
row as fast as I can:

Janmin janmin Ti Kitha Poong'weh
Janmin janmin Ti Kitha Poong'weh
Janmin janmin Ti Kitha Poong'weh

Silence.

A HERALD (*enters and announces*):   The King!

The King and Queen enter preceded by pages, while the orchestra plays Grétry's piece: "Où peut-on être mieux qu'au sein de sa famille?" ("Where is there greater happiness than in the bosom of the family?") At the same time five Africans (males) enter dressed in red, yellow, and green bubas (African robes). The King moves from group to group.

CHRISTOPHE:

Ah! Deliverance! Coronation! Valentine!
John! Sweet William!
Orphans torn from your mothers' breasts.
Yes, my dear friend
Red, yellow, green
The more Stepmother Fortune persecuted them
the more determined I was to clothe them
in the joyous colors of my favor.
Ah, my Mandingos! my Congolese!
I bought them free from the slave ship
redeemed them from infamy.
And to make it known how I delight in them
I've given them a title that makes it clear enough:
The Royal Gumdrops.

A LADY: You have to admit that Royal Gumdrops is adorable.

ANOTHER LADY: Indeed, it would be hard to imagine anything more delicious or more comforting than Royal Gumdrops.

CHRISTOPHE: Lovely ladies, don't be distressed. You too

are royal gumdrops, my dears, the delight of my reign.

Enter GENERAL WARRIOR *and his wife.*

CHRISTOPHE: Speaking of gumdrops, there comes our dear Lady Warrior. Lovelier than ever, but caught cuckolding her king with her Warrior husband. (*Laughing.*) My dear Warrior, I think I'll have to lock you up in the Citadel to put you out of the way.

WARRIOR: I'm not worried, Your Majesty. My wife is virtuous, and you are a little more substantial than a zephyr. I am quite confident that my little Warriors will indeed be little Warriors—to defend you and your crown.

CHRISTOPHE: Well spoken, General. Bah! We're not going to quarrel over a little joke. We still have too many things to do together, haven't we, my friend? For instance, something is going on over there at Saint Marc. We'd better keep our eyes open.

WARRIOR: They're making a big mistake . . . The hand that falls on them won't be a gentle one.

CHRISTOPHE: Thank you, friend, thank you . . . And you, Vastey and Magny, my good friends, what news? Well? What have we been talking about?

MAGNY: We . . . Vastey and I . . . we've been discussing the land question, your Majesty.

CHRISTOPHE: You don't say? So there's a land question? And the King didn't know it? That's a funny thing.

MAGNY: In my opinion, Majesty, there is a question and it's not without urgency. Pétion's agents have been spreading the rumor that he has decided to sell the public lands to private persons.

CHRISTOPHE: Let him, let him. And who's going to buy them? The generals? The rich? The peasants? If it's the rich, I pity the people. And if it's the peasants, I pity the country. Hundreds of tiny plots of sorghum and sweet potatoes. That's anarchy.

Magny, it seems to me that for a general you think too much. (*Menacing.*) A great deal too much.

But there comes our new Archbishop, Monsignor Juan de Dios.

Enter JUAN DE DIOS.

JUAN DE DIOS: Permit me to remind Your Majesty that the Feast of the Assumption is only two weeks off. May I, along with the entire population of the Cape, venture to hope that your Majesty's royal presence will grace our ceremony, one of the most important in the calendar of the Royal Church?

CHRISTOPHE: At the Cape? It's mighty hot at this time of year.

JUAN DE DIOS: Your Majesty, a ceremony of that kind can only be performed with dignity in a cathedral and in a capital city.

CHRISTOPHE: Ho, the cathedral is wherever you are, and the capital is wherever I am.

JUAN DE DIOS: True, Your Majesty, true. Nevertheless it is only at the Cape that we can have all the de-sired pomp.

CHRISTOPHE: Juan de Dios, on August 15th I shall be at Lemonade and nowhere else. If the Blessed Virgin wishes to be celebrated, she had better come too.

He goes out; all follow. JUAN DE DIOS *and* HUGONIN *are last to leave.*

JUAN DE DIOS: Your Majesty, permit me, I must in-sist . . .

HUGONIN: Padre, padre, por favor, don't insist. Ca-ramba, is your head harder than a stone? If the Vir-gen de la Caridad loves us, she can follow us to Lemonade. In Spanish Limonada . . . Comprende Usted esta palabra?

SCENE TWO

~~~~~~~~~~~~~~~~~~~~~~~~~~~~~~~~

The Church at Lemonade. The Feast of the Assumption.
The entire court plus the five Congolese are present. The
King and Queen are kneeling at prie-dieu.

JUAN DE DIOS (alternating with the choir):

JUAN DE DIOS: CHOIR:

    Sancta Maria,   ora pro nobis
    Sancta Dei genetrix,   ora pro nobis
    Mater Christi   ora pro nobis
    Mater divinae gratiae   ora pro nobis

CHRISTOPHE:

    Herzulie Feda Dahomey
    ora pro nobis

JUAN DE DIOS: CHOIR:

    Rosa mystica   ora pro nobis
    Turris Davidica   ora pro nobis
    Turris eburnea   ora pro nobis

CHRISTOPHE:

    Lecco, Petro, Brisé Pimba
    and all the gods of thunder and fire: ora pro nobis.

JUAN DE DIOS: CHOIR:

    Regina Angelorum   ora pro nobis

Regina Patriarcharum   ora pro nobis
Regina Apostolorum   ora pro nobis

CHRISTOPHE:

Zeide Baderre Codonozome—
She stood in the mouths of our cannon and
pointed them—
ora pro nobis.

JUAN DE DIOS:

Agnus Dei qui tollis peccata mundi
Agnus Dei qui tollis peccata mundi
        parce nobis Domine
Agnus Dei qui tollis peccata mundi
        exaudi nos Domine
Agnus Dei qui tollis peccata mundi
        miserere Domine

CHRISTOPHE:

Miserere, miserere.

(Rises as though seeing a ghost and sets his hand on
the Queen's shoulder without looking at her.)

Aah! Don't be afraid, woman
the man who defied St. Peter
isn't afraid of a dying priest, a screeching crow
flying against his sun!

(Threatening an invisible apparition.)

St. Toussaint, who died for our sins,
parce nobis,
St. Dessalines, who died at Red Bridge
like a god caught in a trap—
The black fire of the earth
spewed from the awful cleft
when he with his thunder defied

deceit with the thousand arms.
Miserere
Miserere nobis.

(*The ghost of* CORNEILLE BRELLE *appears against the wall of the church.*)

JUAN DE DIOS: *Oremus. Concede nos famulos tuos, Domine, perpetua mentis et corporis sanitate gaudere. Amen.*

CHRISTOPHE (*standing up and shouting at the priest*):

Juan de Dios, priest of the Roman Church,
What kind of mass is that?

(*Roaring.*)

Corneille Brelle!

(*Collapsing.*)

Damnation! Who has put the Bakula Baka on me?

SCENE THREE

A room in the sacristy. CHRISTOPHE lying in an armchair, his eyes closed. DR. STEWARD and Christophe's retinue are present.

A DISTANT CHOIR:

> Queen of heaven
> And of hell
> Break the chains
> And quench the fires
> Of the awful pit
> Save us from His wrath.

DR. STEWARD: He'll pull through, Madame, thanks to his extraordinary constitution. But brace yourself. He's going to be paralyzed for the rest of his life. Overwork, fatigue, nervous strain, and now this violent shock...

CHRISTOPHE: Paralyzed! . . . Paralyzed? . . . Ah, Steward, is that all your science can do for me?

STEWARD: Your Majesty, we can congratulate ourselves on having prevented the worst . . . Heaven be praised, you are out of danger.

CHRISTOPHE: Prevented the worst? What kind of talk is that? . . . Is there anything worse than being condemned to live when idiot nature has betrayed you? Is there anything worse than surviving yourself? Steward, I'm not fool enough to believe what my cour-

tiers tell me. If I am King, it's not by the grace of
God or the will of the people, but by the will and
the grace of my two fists. Better the butcher's deft
spike. The swift cleaver of death. A clean drop into
nothingness. And you, you, you put up with this
fraud! You let nature take its course. Murderers!
Murderers! You stand there and gape while the
future is being murdered . . .

DISTANT CHOIR:

> Star of the sea
> Of the bitter waters
> Quiet the frothing waves
> Drive death away and guide
> Our quivering ship
> Safely to port.

CHRISTOPHE (*thundering*): Ah, damn it, stop that
infernal hymn singing. And as for those peasants
who have witnessed the crumpling of a king, I advise
them to muzzle their donkeys and gag their chick-
ens. The Lord help the town of Lemonade if I hear
any barnyard noises.

STEWARD: It is true that Your Majesty requires rest and
quiet.

CHRISTOPHE:

> No, gentlemen, no. Come closer.
> I wish to give you my instructions. Come closer,
> I say! I'm not going to eat you, damn it. Good . . .

MINISTERS *and* COURTIERS *gather around the bed.*

> Yes, my knees are crushed. Envious fortune
> has struck me down. But my spirit, believe me,
> is erect, intact, as firm as our Citadel.
> Stricken but unshaken, the living image
> of our Citadel: Christophe.
> I will continue my work.

You will be my limbs, since nature
Denies me the use of my own.
Will any of you decline to buttress
the walls? To sustain the vault and the arches in the
     cyclone?
This is what I expect, gentlemen, what I demand
     of you.
With obedience for its plumbline,
The kingdom will endure by our power.
Let that be known beyond the marshes.
Every man has his rights before God.
And every people.
Gods, I am not begging; in your faces
I shake the scepter of my people—
the hummingbird's beak in the flank of a kite—
For my people I demand its right!
Its share of fortune.

He sinks back exhausted.

SCENE FOUR

~~~~~~

The throne room of the Royal Palace. CHRISTOPHE, *grown old and feeble, in an armchair.* HUGONIN.

HUGONIN (*singing*):

> Damballa plantin' corn dere
> Yessuh, plantin' corn dere
> Fly stung 'is blood dere
> Ah, de nation no good!
> Ah, de nation no good!

CHRISTOPHE (*grown old and feeble*): Ah, Hugonin. Nations are never good. And that's why kings can't be good.

> OFFICERS *enter, come and go. Atmosphere of panic.*

Well what's the news?

FIRST COURIER (*enters*): Not good, Your Majesty.

CHRISTOPHE: I'm asking for the news, not for comments on the news. Prézeau, call Richard. He can't be very far away, and we might need him. Well?

FIRST COURIER: Our forces were on the point of taking Saint-Marc. Thereupon the rebels sent an appeal to the republicans. General Boyer has landed in Saint-Marc. (*Exit.*)

CHRISTOPHE: Thunderation! I held out the olive branch to those people in Port-au-Prince. And they've refused it. For five years now we've had peace on the

frontiers, now they want blood. Very well, gentlemen. Suit yourselves. You say that Boyer has entered
Saint-Marc? And under the noses of my generals!

Enter a second COURIER.

SECOND COURIER: Your Majesty, Generals Roman and
Warrior have deserted to the rebels. (*Exit.*)

CHRISTOPHE: Ha! Roman. Warrior. My generals. Swine.
Horned serpents. Men I've showered with honors.
Take care, gentlemen. Christophe is a hard nut to
crack. Prézeau, inform Magny that he is to take
command.

HUGONIN: Your Majesty, Caradeux is a handsome estate
not far from Port-au-Prince. If I'm not misinformed,
the Senate in Port-au-Prince has just made Magny
a present of it. Magny has always had an eye for
land, Your Majesty.

PRÉZEAU *enters but remains in the background.*

CHRISTOPHE: Swine, the whole lot of them! What a
dung heap this country is! Manure steaming in the
sun! I can see Jehovah sniffing!
Magny, Warrior, Roman!
Well, we'll get along without them, won't we?
No use making mountains out of mole hills.
A few struts give way. A few stones break loose. But
the vaulting is intact. Intact, do you hear! Intact!
Send me Richard.

THIRD COURIER (*enters*):   Your Majesty. The population
has risen at the Cape, the mob has seized the
Arsenal.

CHRISTOPHE: But what about the garrison? And
Richard?

THIRD COURIER: The rioters are spreading the rumor
that Governor Richard has no intention of resisting.
(*Exit.*)

CHRISTOPHE: But where is Richard?

RICHARD *enters*.

Ah, Count of the Northern Marches, I was beginning to wonder if you'd come. And here you are. I'm glad to see that you still fear me. The Cape is in revolt and you, the Governor, know nothing about it?

RICHARD: Your Majesty, I won't deny that the situation is extremely serious.

CHRISTOPHE: Ha, you won't deny . . . Out of my sight, you traitor. But before you go, damn your soul, get down on your knees and kiss your master's hands.

RICHARD *complies and exits*.

SCENE FIVE

HUGONIN, CHRISTOPHE, and an AFRICAN PAGE squatting on his heels and looking up at the King.

HUGONIN:

> One, two little branches
> He put his foot on the twig
> What's that game the kid is playing?
> Hell, it's the capon game.

CHRISTOPHE: What's that idiotic song, Hugonin?
HUGONIN: I learned it a long time ago in Santo Domingo. And here's another:
(*Singing*):

> Rinfofo
> And Rinfofo
> Drumstick hot, drumstick cold
> Dry meat and beans, no good!

CHRISTOPHE: That's enough comic relief. "Sow your rocky soil with Ambition," I said, and raised the water level in the canals ten notches. We measured our harvests in sweat. Those were harsh times. I regret nothing. I tried to put something into an inhospitable land.
HUGONIN: And . . . look at the land now . . . Columns

of smoke are rising . . . Wind . . . the neighing of horses. The King's fields are burning.

CHRISTOPHE: I tried to give them hunger for action.

HUGONIN: Hunger, my oh my! And now they're eating the King's hams and swilling the King's wine; all they leave behind is their beastly rancid smell in the midst of the King's perfumes.

CHRISTOPHE: Smash, ruin, destroy. I garnered grain for them, garnered for envy and wind. For dust and ruin.

HUGONIN: The people live from day to day, Your Majesty.

CHRISTOPHE: I tried to unfold the enigma of this backward people.

HUGONIN: Each people has its own pace, Your Majesty, its secret pace.

CHRISTOPHE: Damnation! Other peoples had time to build step by short step, over the centuries. Our only hope is to take long steps, year by groaning year.

HUGONIN: Listen, Your Majesty. Smell, breathe the air. It's a feast day on the heights of the Cape. The peasants' cauldrons are bubbling. Out in the open, covered with banana leaves.

CHRISTOPHE: Faugh. Your voice is strange, Hugonin. Every one of your words is weighed down with the wreckage of my dreams. Because they were carried from their homes and spat on, I tried to give them a place in the world; I tried to teach them how to build their houses, how to stand up as free men.

HUGONIN: And now I hear the beating of drums . . . Your soldiers aren't standing up. The King's soldiers are beating the mandoucouman.

CHRISTOPHE: By God, they are! The scoundrels! They're beating the mandoucouman.

During this speech THE PAGE *stands up, circles round the King and bends toward him.*

AFRICAN PAGE: What does it mean, Your Majesty?

CHRISTOPHE: Ah! It means that it's time for the old king to lie down. No God, no gods, only the night; night of the narrow muzzle, night of the hunt, night of fugitive blacks, night of bitter salt, night of the dog. (THE PAGE *returns to his squatting position and looks up at him with devotion.*) Night unique in the procession of nights, night that obliterates the shape and the scar; night which I know, because you are the monkey bread from the great baobab of time; almond sprung from the harsh flint of days; night of grass and roots; night of springs, night of the scor-
pion,
I'm coming and you won't see me stumbling.
Yes, Congo.
You have, we have, a proverb that says:
"When you see an arrow that's not going to miss you, throw out your chest and meet it head on." You hear me? Head on.

Addresses THE PAGE *directly.*

Congo, I've often watched
the impetuous hummingbird in the datura blossom
and wondered how so frail a body can hold
that hammering heart without bursting.
Africa, rouse my blood with your big horn
Make it open like a giant bird.
Ah, cage of my chest, don't burst
Beat, drums of my heart.
The toucan cracks the fruit of the raffia palm with
his beak:
Hail, toucan, great drummer.

Cock, the night bleeds at the ax-edge of your cry:
Hail, cock, toiling ax.
Snapping at pennants, blade by blade,
the kingfisher composes a banner of drunken sun-
       light:
Hail kingfisher, great drummer.
Cock drum, toucan drum, kingfisher drum
drum of my blood
Drum, drum, my heart.
My children, when I die, the big drum will stop.
So let it beat while it beats, let the big drum
beat a river of blood for me
a hurricane of blood and life.
My body!

THE QUEEN *is heard singing in Creole.* CHRISTOPHE
*stands up and takes a few steps to the balcony. The
troops burst out cheering when he appears.*

CHRISTOPHE:
       Thank you, my friends, thank you.
       Sound the assembly. Summon all my troops!

PRÉZEAU *brings him his cloak and his two-cornered
hat.*

       Every last man! My guards! My cavalry!
       Saddle my horse. Do they think I can't fight any
              more?
       Bah! Papa Christophe has only to show the corners
              of his hat
       on the heights of the Cape, and they'll all go crawl-
              ing home.
SOLDIERS (*six or seven soldiers under arms enter*):   Hur-
       rah! Hurrah! Hurrah!
CHRISTOPHE:
       Men, you will be fighting an army of riffraff

The army of disorder, neglect, laziness
Led by a young fop whose only title to glory
Was won in Pétion's bed.
We have built. They will destroy.
Riffraff? No, worms.
Soft-bodied, gluttonous termites.
Are you all ready to defend the house that shelters
   you
Your tutelary tree,
Your King
Against a wretched army of termites?

SOLDIERS: Hurrah! Hurrah!

CHRISTOPHE: Then forward! (*He falls.*) Damnation!
Who did that? What invisible enemy is camped at
the foot of my walls?

BOYER (*suddenly appears in the background. The un-
realistic character of this apparition should be
stressed*):   At last the iron mace he brandished over
your heads is breaking in his hands . . . His own
lieutenants are abandoning him, sick of being no
more than the first among his slaves. Vengeance
roused from the heart of Providence is hot in pur-
suit of him. Soldiers of the Republic, you are the
soldiers of God.

SOLDIERS: Hurrah! Hurrah! Hurrah! (*They cross the
stage and follow* BOYER.)

CHRISTOPHE (*being helped up by* HUGONIN, PRÉZEAU, *and*
THE PAGE):   Africa, help me to go home, carry me
like an aged child in your arms. Undress me and
wash me. Strip me of all these garments, strip me as
a man strips off dreams when the dawn comes . . .
Strip me of my nobles, my nobility, my scepter, my
crown. And wash me, oh, wash me clean of their
grease paint, their kisses, wash me clean of my kingdom. I'll attend to the rest alone.

He takes the little revolver that hangs on a chain from his neck.

The curtain falls and rises on Scene Six. Against a background of ruins and desolation enters HUGONIN, *dressed in black swallowtails and a top hat.*

SCENE SIX

<hr>

Half-darkness. Empty stage. HUGONIN *enters in evening dress, white gloves, a wooden cross on his top hat. The spotlight follows him as he moves.*

HUGONIN:

> Oh, that rum! Maybe I've had a little too much.
> That tiger piss!
> Forgive me, ladies and gentlemen, if I'm a little late.
> I'm the character who always comes in at the end.
> And remember, I've all these blessed doodads to put
> on.
> My tailcoat, my top hat, and, oh, I'd almost for-
> gotten . . . my specters. Oh that rum, you know
> what I mean, my spectacles! Well, I've made it—
> that's the main thing—we're all on time for the
> minute of silence.
> You heard me: minute of silence.
> Attention please:

> *His voice becomes more and more dramatic.*

> While the soldiers fasten palm fronds to their
> shakos; while the barons and dukes turn their coats
> as fast as they can—

> *A pistol shot is heard.* HUGONIN *gasps and stands in
> silence for a moment. Then he removes his hat and
> speaks with sober dignity.*

I remain your humble servant
Bernard Justus Hugonin
Sometimes addressed as Baron Saturday.

Stooped over, he exits very slowly rear; the spotlight follows him.

SCENE SEVEN

~~~~~~

Construction site in the mountains. Scaffolding.

FIRST ECHO: The King is dead . . .
SECOND ECHO: The King is dead . . .

> PEASANTS, *men and women, enter from one side carrying the body. From the other side enter* VASTEY, THE QUEEN, *who is dressed very simply in white, and* THE AFRICAN PAGE. *The three stand together on the side.*

VASTEY:
Stand him upright in the mortar.
Turned southward. That's good. Not lying down.
Standing. Le him make his own way amid hardship,
rock and the industry of human hands.
And when by his own resources he has found his
stature
Let the red moon hang its terrible torch
on the pinnacle of the tower.

THE QUEEN:
And this country will have refused you
so much as the toad's pillow of moss
And your country will have denied you
the scarab's cave of mud.
Man, extender of boundary-stones
Man, forger of stars

94

Hard, hot embrace
Great dedicated heart, so soon grown cold in the
    distance
Put off your stony pride
and think of a little old woman
who will hobble through dust and rain
in the cracked daylight to glean
your name till journey's end.

THE AFRICAN PAGE:

Father, we establish you in the holy city, on the hill
    of the three palm trees.
Father, we establish you amid the sixteen circuits
    of the wind
Here sleep patience and impatience
Victory and defeat—
Imbricated scales in the dim light—
Slumber of arms
slumber of tears.
Power of night, tide of the day
Shango
I salute you. O . . . . . as you ride
through the halls of heaven
mounted on the flaming ram of the tempest.

VASTEY (*addressing the King*):

King, on our shoulders we have brought you
through the mountains at the height of the floods
to this place.
For your path had a name:
Thirst-of-the-Mountain.
And here you are again, a king erect
holding your own memorial tablet over the abyss.
O fragile-hearted stars
born of the pyre of Ethiopian Memnon
O pollen-swarming birds

fashion for him imperishable arms:
on azure field red phoenix crowned with gold.

Funereal fanfares, cannon salutes.

CURTAIN .